SOUTHERN COUNTIES
from the air

PHOTOGRAPHED BY
Denny Rowland

TEXT BY
John Mannion

MYRIAD
LONDON

First published in 2005 by
Myriad Books Limited
35 Bishopsthorpe Road
London SE26 4PA

ISBN 1 904 736 89 0

Designed by Jerry Goldie
Graphic Design

Printed in China

www.myriadbooks.com

Previous page: Chesil Beach,
Dorset; right: Brighton

Southern Counties from the air

THE SOUTHERN COUNTIES is a region of England very much like a large piece of parchment that has been written on, had sections erased, and then been written on again. The first marks on the landscape are those created by the sea, the wind and the rain. Well-loved features such as the White Cliffs of Dover, Lulworth Cove, the Needles or Old Harry's Rocks are the result of the ceaseless pressure of the elements. They all now appear permanent but in time will alter and eventually disappear under the ravages of the weather.

The second marks on the landscape are those produced by people. Iron Age forts have given way to Roman citadels which have in turn been replaced by Norman castles or Tudor manor houses. Large parts of the southern counties that we see today are the products of the Regency and Victorian eras but the process of human development seems as relentless as that of the weather. New landmarks such as the Spinnaker Tower in Portsmouth or the Bluewater Shopping Centre in Kent are constantly springing up to replace the piers and winter gardens of a previous age.

Before aircraft, the desire for a better view and a fuller understanding of the landscape had to be satisfied by physically climbing to a high vantage point such as Box Hill in Surrey. Now, aerial photography allows the viewer to see how things fit together in a way that is not possible from a close-up shot taken from the ground. Cliffs are imposing if viewed from below, or frightening if viewed from the top but only in an aerial photograph can you see how the cliff relates to the land beyond it or how it has affected human settlement. On a smaller scale you can look at individual houses or even rows of houses from the ground but only from the air can you see the pattern of the streets that differentiate the planned and unplanned phases of a town's development – Brighton, for example.

Viewing the English countryside from the air offers a new perspective and this collection of stunning photographs of the southern counties will give readers a fresh insight into the region as a whole as it sweeps from the gentle agricultural heartland of Kent and Surrey to the more rugged landscapes of Dorset.

John Mannion

Contents

KENT

KENT, THE GARDEN OF ENGLAND, is rich with idyllic countryside, historic towns and coastal resorts. As England's closest point to the Continent it was the starting point of Julius Caesar's invasion and the place where Hengist and Horsa, the first of the Angles, Saxons and Jutes, landed. As the guardian of the approaches to the Thames, the county has a long tradition of naval excellence, typified by the royal dockyards at Chatham. It was the centre of the Christian conversion of England and Canterbury Cathedral remains one of the country's finest Christian monuments. In more recent times Kent's proximity to the Continent has led to its development as a transport hub which includes the Dover Ferry port and the Channel Tunnel terminal at Ashford.

THE DOVER FERRY TERMINAL
The Port of Dover is the country's leading cross-channel ferry port and the busiest in northern Europe. Over 1.6m freight vehicles, 3m cars and 18m passengers use the terminal each year. The eastern side of the harbour is the main passenger terminal and has berths for seven ferries.

WHITE CLIFFS
The chalky soils of Kent are cut off dramatically at Dover and provide one of England's most instantly recognisable natural landmarks. The White Cliffs of Dover rise above the English Channel to heights of over 300ft (91m) in places and stretch for 10 miles (16km) between Walmer to the east and Folkestone to the west. Their dramatic presence has inspired artists from Shakespeare to Vera Lynn and they have witnessed events such as the first cross-channel flight by Louis Bleriot in 1909 and the first cross-channel swim by Captain Matthew Webb in 1875. The Gateway to the White Cliffs visitor centre has recently been opened by the National Trust.

DOVER CASTLE

Sir Walter Raleigh summed up the military nature of Dover when speaking to Elizabeth I: "No promontory town or haven of Christendom is so placed by nature and situation both to gratify friends and annoy enemies as this your majesty's town of Dover." There have been castles at Dover since the Iron Age, although the present building dates mostly from the time of Henry II. The castle sits on top of the White Cliffs but beneath it are a vast network of underground tunnels whose construction began in the Middle Ages. They were greatly extended during the Napoleonic Wars, amid fears of a French invasion, and last saw use in the Second World War.

FORENESS POINT
(right)

Foreness Point near Broadstairs is the most south-easterly point in mainland Britain. There has been a lighthouse nearby since 1505 and in 1899 Marconi set up one of the earliest wireless telegraphy stations there. The point's location makes it a favoured port of call for seabirds and, of course, birdwatchers.

DEAL CASTLE *(left)*

Deal Castle was commissioned by Henry VIII in 1539 because of fears of an invasion by European Catholic powers. Along with Walmer and Sandown it formed part of a defensive line known as the "castles in the Downs". Unlike medieval castles, which had high outer walls to maximise their archers' range, Deal Castle has low, thick walls to provide protection against heavy guns. The castle's cylindrical bastions surrounding a circular tower are also tailored to the needs of gunners. The castle was built to house a military garrison rather than a family. Deal Castle was a royalist stronghold during the Civil War. It was besieged from July 12 to August 25 1648 but surrendered on news of the collapse of Royalist resistance elsewhere.

SANDGATE (right)

Sandgate is a village between Folkestone and Hythe. It was once a vital part of the country's coastal defences and there are six Napoleonic era Martello towers in the area. On the beach is a castle built by Henry VIII which has been much reduced by time and tide. In the 18th century Sandgate provided shipbuilding facilities for George III's navy and it had a brief period as a fashionable retreat before the development of Folkestone and Hythe. Nowadays Sandgate is an important centre for the antiques trade.

FOLKESTONE (above)

Without a river or deepwater harbour Folkestone was little more than a lookout post for the Romans but a church and castle were built there during the Anglo-Saxon period around which the fishing village of Folkestone coalesced. The town grew in importance during the middle ages but its fishermen were not above attacking passing merchantmen for plunder. In the 18th century the village became a famous centre for smuggling. Respectability arrived in the 19th century when a new harbour was built and the railways enabled it to become a popular seaside resort.

SALTWOOD CASTLE (right)

Saltwood Castle is a 12th-century Norman building that was added to and extended over a 200-year period. In 1580 an earthquake struck the castle rendering it uninhabitable. It was restored in the 19th century, and has remained in private hands since then. The gatehouse is used as the principal residence. Two of the most famous owners of the castle were the art historian and broadcaster Sir Kenneth Clark and his son Alan, the politician and diarist.

THE ROYAL MILITARY CANAL

The Royal Military Canal was built in 1804 as a third line of defence, after the navy and the Martello tower system, against an invading Napoleonic army. The canal provided military transport as well as forming a defensive barrier. Guard houses were built at all the bridges and it was hoped that these would do something to quell the smuggling that flourished in the area. The canal was re-fortified during World War II.

APPLEDORE

Appledore is situated on the edge of the Romney Marsh. For such a small town Appledore has seen a great deal of action. It was a headquarters for the Danes when they invaded in 892, the French invaded and sacked the town in 1380 and the men of Appledore joined in both the Peasant's Revolt and Jack Cade's rebellion. The military canal, built in response to Napoleon's invasion plans, lies between the town and the sea.

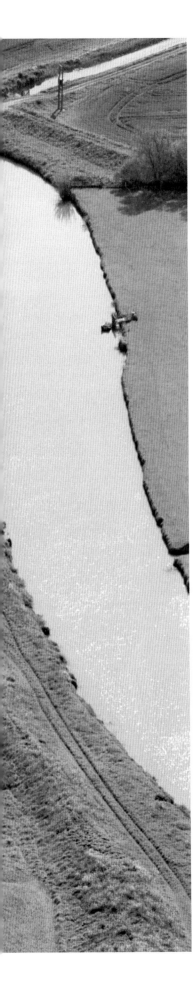

THE CHANNEL TUNNEL

The idea of a tunnel under the English Channel has been around since the Napoleonic period, and has been technically feasible for almost a hundred years. Digging began for the present tunnel in 1987-88 and was completed in 1991. The tunnel was officially opened in May 1994. This remarkable feat of engineering does not always get the recognition it deserves because so much of it is underground. Only the two severely functional entrances can be seen by the casual observer.

BLUEWATER

Bluewater, near Dartford, is a giant retail park which opened for business in March 1999. It is triangular in shape with a large department store at each corner. As well as shopping facilities Bluewater can feed 5000 people at a time and provide parking for 13,000 cars. A 12-screen cinema, gyms and family areas are amongst the site's entertainment facilities. It was built on the site of a former chalk quarry and over a million trees and shrubs went into the creation of the 53 acres of parkland that surround the centre.

GILLINGHAM FC

Gillingham FC is the only football club in the county of Kent to maintain a place in the Football League. The club was founded in 1893 and reached the first division 107 years later in 2000. The club plays at Priestfield Stadium where the pitch is 114 yards long and 77 yards wide (104m x 70m).

BRANDS HATCH

Brands Hatch began life in 1926. It is situated in a natural bowl that provides good all-round views. Nigel Mansell won his first Formula One Grand Prix at Brands Hatch in 1985. It is no longer used as an F1 circuit.

CARS AT SHEERNESS

Around half a million cars are imported via Sheerness each year and there are 290 acres of dedicated car storage areas around the port.

ASHFORD SHOPPING

McArthur Glen is built on the site of a former railway works. It was designed by Sir Richard Rogers and is intended to evoke a medieval encampment. Its architect described it as "a Bedouin tent in an English meadow".

HISTORIC DOCKYARD CHATHAM

Chatham Dockyard is sited on the east bank of the river Medway, on a narrow stretch of the river just before it snakes out into the estuary on its way into the outer reaches of the Thames. Commissioned by Henry VIII the royal docks were the birthplace of the British Navy: numerous warships including Nelson's famous flagship *HMS Victory* were built at Chatham and, by the outbreak of the Second World War, over 13,000 people worked at the docks. By the late 1960s the docks were being run down and closure was eventually announced in June 1981. Now the dockyard and its splendid Georgian buildings have been successfully restored as a huge museum charting the colourful history of British shipbuilding in the age of sail.

UPNOR CASTLE

Upnor Castle was built in the 16th century to protect warships anchored in the Medway. This function explains its unusual design. At the front of the castle there is a triangular bastion which is further protected by a wooden palisade. The castle is strongest towards the river, although a moat and landward gate were added towards the end of the 16th century.

YALDING

Yalding, a small village about five miles (8km) from Maidstone, is recorded in the Domesday Book. Its name is derived from the Anglo-Saxon for "old village". The village is near the confluence of the rivers Medway and Beult and features one of the longest medieval stone bridges in England. Town Bridge is about 450ft (137m) long and was constructed in the 1400s, probably on the site of an older wooden structure. During the Civil War, in 1643, a party of Royalists attempted to advance from Aylesford towards Tonbridge via Yalding, but were cut off by Parliamentarians at Town Bridge. After a bombardment 300 Royalists surrendered.

HEVER CASTLE

Famed as the childhood home of Anne Boleyn (1507-1536), Hever Castle is a Tudor mansion built on top of a much older 13th-century structure. The central Tudor manor house was built by the Boleyn family around 1500 whilst the stone gatehouse and outer walls date from the 13th century. The whole complex is surrounded by a double moat. King Henry VIII wooed Anne Boleyn at Hever Castle but after marrying and then beheading her, he gave the castle to his fourth wife, Anne of Cleves. Hever Castle was purchased by William Waldorf Astor, the American millionaire, in 1903 and greatly restored. Amongst other things Astor added an Italian garden, a rose garden, a maze and a 35-acre lake. A Tudor herb garden was planted in 1994.

LEEDS CASTLE, KENT (left)

There has been a castle on this island in a lake since 857. The present building was begun in 1119 but it was largely rebuilt and extended by Edward I, who added a barbican and the D-shaped tower known as the "gloriette" on the smaller of the two islands in the lake. The castle was popular with the queens of England during the middle ages and was the residence of Eleanor and Margaret, the two wives of Edward I, Philippa of Hainhault, the wife of Edward III, Catherine de Valois, Henry V's wife and Catherine of Aragon, first wife of Henry VIII. Elizabeth I was briefly imprisoned at the castle before she became queen. The fortress was extensively modernised and made more luxurious under Henry VIII. Work began in 1517 and parts of the present banqueting hall date from that time. Much of the castle was restored and rebuilt in the 19th century.

SISSINGHURST

Little now remains of the splendid moated Tudor manor house visited by both Mary I and Elizabeth I. The central tower survives almost unchanged from the Tudor period but the rest of the mansion fell into disrepair in the 17th century. During the Seven Years War the manor was used to house French prisoners in deeply miserable conditions. Sissinghurst was on the point of being demolished when, in 1930, the writer and gardener Vita Sackville-West and her husband, Harold Nicolson, bought it. Apart from careful restoration the new owners made few changes to the house but they completely transformed the grounds to create one of England's most popular gardens.

CANTERBURY CATHEDRAL

Canterbury became one of the earliest centres of Christianity in Britain when St Augustine made it his missionary base in 597 AD. Various churches have stood on the site but the present building, which was begun in the 11th century, combines a mixture of Gothic and Perpendicular styles. On December 29 1170 archbishop Thomas à Beckett was murdered by four knights who thought they were carrying out the wishes of King Henry II. The archbishop was instantly declared a martyr and Canterbury became one of the most popular destinations for pilgrimage in the Middle Ages. Canterbury remains the premier see in Britain and the present Archbishop is the 104th.

TONBRIDGE

Tonbridge owes its existence to its favourable position on the River Medway and has been a centre of trade and transport since Anglo-Saxon times. A 13th-century motte and bailey castle dominates the town which also contains some well-preserved Elizabethan timber-framed buildings and fine 18th-century weatherboarded and tiled houses. Tonbridge School, founded in 1553, sits at the top of the town.

BEDGEBURY CROSS

Bedgebury is chiefly remarkable for the Bedgebury Pinetum which houses the National Conifer Collection. This was established at Bedgebury in 1925, as the atmosphere at London's Kew Gardens was considered too polluted for conifer planting. The collection has over 6,241 tree specimens growing in 320 acres, including rare, historically important and endangered trees. It also contains some of the oldest and largest examples of conifers in Britain.

FINCHCOCKS *(above)*

The house at Finchcocks was substantially completed in 1725 as a residence for a successful barrister. It cost around £30,000 to build. It suffered the not uncommon fate of many large houses, changing hands on a number of occasions and gradually losing its grounds to developers and local farmers. During the Second World War the house was home to 24 evacuated schoolboys and in the 1960s it was a ballet school. In 1971 it was acquired by its present owner, the pianist and collector, Richard Burnett. The house is now open to the public and houses a substantial collection of historical keyboard instruments such as early pianos, chamber organs, harpsichords, virginals, spinets and clavichords.

KNOLE PARK *(below)*

Knole Park began life as a residence for the Archbishop of Canterbury in 1456 but eventually it was given to Henry VIII. In 1566 Queen Elizabeth I passed the house on to Thomas Sackville, 1st Earl of Dorset, whose descendants continue to live there. The house was reconstructed between 1603 and 1608 but has not changed significantly since. During the Civil War it was sacked but restored shortly afterwards when the 5th Earl married Lady Frances Cranfield who brought furniture, tapestries and paintings from Copt Hall, her home in Essex. The 6th Earl, as Lord Chamberlain to William III, had the right to any furnishings discarded from the royal palaces and was thus able to continue the family's collection of furniture. Knole was the birthplace of Vita Sackville-West, and is said to have inspired Virginia Woolf's historical fantasy *Orlando*. Knole is set in a 1,000-acre deer park.

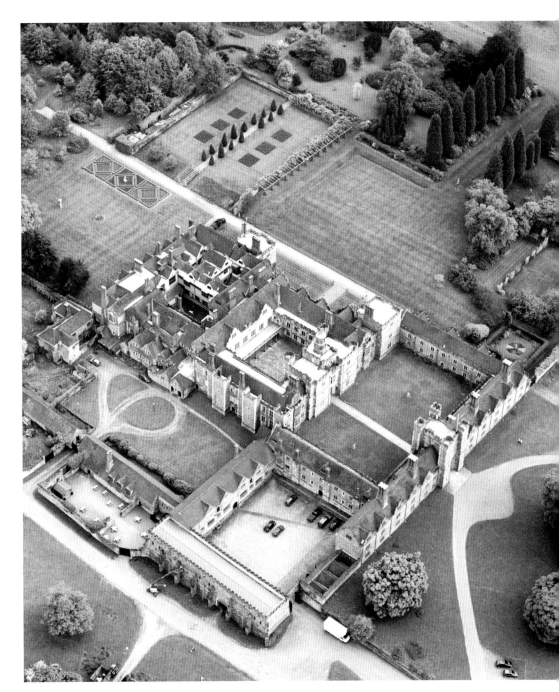

PENSHURST PLACE *(above)*

The early history of Penshurst Place is somewhat turbulent as three of its owners were beheaded as traitors to the crown. The building dates back to the 13th century but it reached its period of greatest prosperity when the house was given to Sir William Sidney by Edward VI. Sir William's grandson was the soldier, scholar and poet Sir Philip Sidney, who became the first commoner to be given a state funeral at St Paul's Cathedral after his death at the battle of Zutphen. The house remains in the hands of the Sydney family today.

SCOTNEY CASTLE *(left)*

At the centre of the Scotney estate and gardens stands Scotney Castle. The original castle was begun in 1378 during a period of French coastal raids. It was altered during the Elizabethan and Jacobean eras but then fell into disrepair. In 1837 a new manor house was begun and the old castle left as a feature of the gardens, widely regarded as among the most romantic in England.

ALLINGTON CASTLE

The first castle at Allington, near Maidstone, was little more than a large mound and some wooden walls but a more substantial stone building was raised during the reign of Edward I. A distinctive herringbone pattern in the stonework can still be seen in the oldest parts of the castle. By the 15th century the castle, which never saw action, had become a fortified mansion. A disastrous fire at the beginning of the 17th century reduced large stretches of the castle to rubble and the remains barely amounted to more than a large farmhouse. The explorer Sir Martin Conway extensively restored Allington in the early 20th century and in 1951 the site became a Carmelite convent.

BEWL WATER

Set in an area of outstanding natural beauty Bewl Water reservoir is the largest stretch of open water in south-east England. It is situated in the High Weald on the border between Kent and Sussex and it provides a habitat for a wide range of wildlife. The reservoir is also a popular centre for recreation and has facilities for sailing, windsurfing, fishing, cycling and walking.

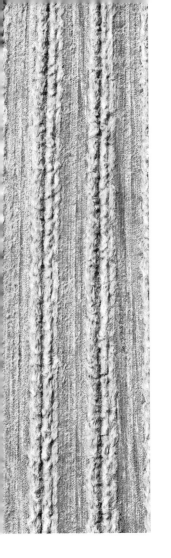

WHITBREAD HOP FARM

Although Kent is often described as the Garden of England few people stop to wonder what is growing in the garden. The rich and varied soils of Kent provide opportunities for all types of agriculture from fruit-growing to sheep-farming, but perhaps the most characteristic Kentish crop is the hop, a staple product of beer-making. Whitbread Hop Farm (above), was owned by the famous brewing family for over 70 years from the 1920s to the 1990s. From 1984 onwards it has been converted into a heritage centre to illustrate the hop-picking industry. There are five oast houses in the complex as well as a hop garden and a home for shire horses. Numerous exhibitions illustrate the history of the crop and the area.

PFIZER HEADQUARTERS

Pfizer, the largest pharmaceutical company in the UK, has its headquarters just outside the ancient port of Sandwich. The site covers 340 acres and employs about 3600 staff. Of these around 2700 work on the research and development of medicines, as well as consumer health products. Pfizer's modern, energy-efficient building has grown in stages since the company first moved to Sandwich in 1957.

SUSSEX

SUSSEX has a long history of involvement in conflict and war: Saxon rule of England came to an end at the Battle of Hastings and in the middle ages the county provided enthusiastic supporters for both the Peasant's Revolt and Jack Cade's rebellion. One of the natural treasures of Sussex is the South Downs which enter the county from the west and run for 50 miles (80km) to their terminus at Beachy Head. Most of the hills are above 500ft (150m) and Ditchling Beacon, the highest point on the Downs in Sussex, is over 814ft (248m). The strategic importance of Sussex and its proximity to London mean that the county is well supplied with a large collection of picturesque castles, stately homes and historic towns.

HOVE KING ALFRED

This leisure complex was completed in 1939; its design was ahead of its time and included an underground car park at a time when there were few private cars.

CUCKMERE HAVEN

The river Cuckmere reaches the sea at Cuckmere Haven after following a meandering course through its beautiful lower valley. There are fine walks along the shingle beach and classic views of the Seven Sisters. The Haven may look peaceful today but it was once a hotbed of smuggling. The remains of the German sailing vessel *Polynesia*, which sank in 1890, can still be seen at low tide.

BRIGHTON PAVILION

The Prince Regent (later King George IV) first visited Brighton in 1783 on the advice of his surgeon that the seawater there would be good for his gout. The Prince enjoyed the area so much that he decided to build his own grand seaside residence in the town. The first phase was designed by Henry Holland but the building did not acquire its maharajah's palace look until John Nash took over. The second phase was completed in 1822. After the death of George VI Queen Victoria sold the Pavilion to the local council and during the First World War it was used as a military hospital.

BRIGHTON TOWN CENTRE *(right)*

For most of its early history Brighton was a small fishing village but its fortunes changed radically from the mid 18th century when sea-bathing became fashionable. The seawater at Brighton was thought to be particularly beneficial and when Dr Richard Russell of Lewes set up a spa in the town, the sick and the infirm – but most importantly the rich – quickly beat a path to his door. The sudden influx of wealth is reflected in the Regency terraces that were built in the 1780s. Brighton's status was raised even higher when the Prince Regent became a regular visitor and constructed the exotic Royal Pavilion.

BRIGHTON'S HISTORY

The history of the town can easily be understood by studying a street map. The original fishing village with its small streets and tiny plots is now an area known as the Lanes – although most of the original fisherman's homes have long since disappeared. The Lanes is now a centre for Brighton's antique shops and is packed with small bars and restaurants. The town's period of prosperity in the 18th and early 19th centuries can be glimpsed in the wider roads and imposing buildings of the Regency and Victorian eras. And Brighton's grand railway station bears testament to the importance of the railway in Brighton's development.

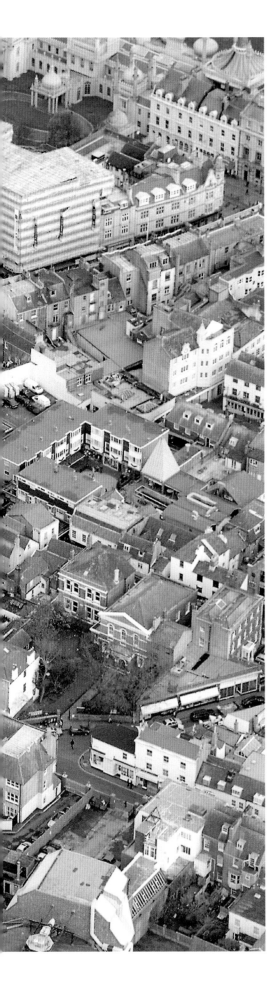

BRIGHTON & HOVE

With prosperity comes expansion. The original town of Brighton and its near neighbour Hove now form a single conurbation which was granted city status in the year 2000. The two communities remain distinct however and Brighton is generally considered to be livelier than Hove. This may be due to the large number of young people in Brighton, which has two universities and plays host to thousands of foreign students. The lively youth scene may also account for the large number of bars in the town – there are said to be over 365 places to drink. On the other hand there are also more than 50 churches for the more sober-minded inhabitants. Famously Brighton was the scene of clashes between Mods and Rockers in the 1960s.

BRIGHTON'S PIERS

Brighton has two piers. The oldest is the West Pier which was built in 1863 and is one of only two Grade I listed piers in the UK. It was originally designed as a promenade pier but screens and a pavilion were added in the 1890s. The pavilion was converted to a theatre in 1903 and to an amusement arcade in 1945. By the early 1970s it was in serious need of repair and it was proposed that the south end should be demolished. This plan was never carried out. The West Pier was closed for renovation in 1975 and since then it has suffered a series of disasters including partial collapses in 2002 and 2003 and two fires in 2003. All that now remains of the structure are its original cast iron frames.

The Palace Pier, now known as Brighton Pier, was begun in 1891 and opened in 1899. It was one of the last British piers to be built and is 1,760ft (536m) long. It included a 1,500-seater pavilion at the seaward end as well as smaller pavilions along its length containing restaurants together with smoking and reading rooms. Ornamental arches were provided for the electrical illuminations and an electric tramway ran up the centre. It was extended in 1938 but was closed as a precaution two years later during the war: local legend has it that the authorities feared it could be used as a runway for enemy planes. In 1973, work to demolish the pier's unused landing stage was underway when a gale caused heavy damage. Repairs were undertaken but the pier's original theatre had to be dismantled. The idea was to store the building ready for restoration; in the ensuing period the theatre was lost and its location is still unknown.

SUNSET, BRIGHTON MARINA

Brighton Marina is the largest purpose-built harbour for yachts and sailing boats in the United Kingdom. It is an ideal starting point both for coastal sailing to neighbouring places such as Beachy Head and the Seven Sisters or cross-channel trips. Sea walls enclose two jetties that provide accommodation for every kind of craft from dinghies to luxury yachts and the deep-water entrance to the marina ensures that sailors have 24-hour access to the sea. As well as sailing, charter boats are available at the marina for fishing and diving expeditions.

THE UNDERCLIFF, BRIGHTON MARINA

Alongside the marina there is an extensive leisure complex which contains a yacht club, cinema, casino, a health and fitness club, bowling alley and a wide variety of waterfront shops, bars and restaurants. Across the Channel, sailors can visit the attractive fishing port of Fecamp, 65 miles (104km) away. For those of a non-nautical persuasion the Undercliff path starts at the marina and runs along the bottom of the chalk cliffs to Saltdean. The path is completely flat and is particularly popular with cyclists.

BRIGHTON STATION

Brighton railway station was opened for use in May 1840 but the terminus building was not completed until September 1841, in time for the opening of the main line from London. The original station building was in an Italianate style and was the work of David Mocatta who designed all the stations on the London to Brighton line. Brighton is the only surviving example of his work, although later additions to the station have obscured some of the original façade. When the station opened, the *Brighton Gazette* commented, "The Brighton terminus is a beautiful structure, and with the iron sheds in the rear, will not suffer from comparison with any railway terminus in existence." The elegant cast iron and glass train shed was erected between 1882 and 1883: it is 75ft (23m) high and was constructed without disturbing the train timetable. The railway brought greater prosperity to Brighton than even the patronage of the Prince Regent. The town was now within easy reach of London and, as the 19th century progressed, more and more people had the money and leisure time to take advantage of Brighton's seaside attractions.

BRIGHTON RACES *(right)*

Racing arrived at Brighton at the same period as the resort became fashionable and began to receive royal patronage. The first race took place in August 1783 and the Prince Regent attended his first meeting there in September. The money for constructing the course was raised by subscription as was the money for the stand which was added in 1788. Racing at Brighton has sometimes had a chequered history: in 1805 part of the course was ploughed up by a local landowner who believed that the racing authorities owed him 100 guineas; in 1848, a riot, a whirlwind, and an invasion of the grandstand all took place in the same week. In spite of these mishaps, Brighton has developed a reputation as a popular and informal racecourse.

PALMEIRA SQUARE
HOVE *(left)*

Palmeira Square was built in 1855 as an extension of Adelaide Crescent which had been completed in 1850. The site had originally been intended for a glass and cast iron conservatory which anticipated the Crystal Palace in its design. The architect Amon Wilds supervised the early stages of the work but resigned when a central supporting column was removed from the design. The building collapsed a day after it had been completed. Although firmly Victorian in date the two long terraces and their central park are Regency in style.

HOVE

Due to expansion, Hove and Brighton now form a single conurbation and are often referred to as "Brighton and Hove" as if they were one single entity. Hove was very much a latecomer to the scene compared to Brighton. At the beginning of the 19th century its population was just 101; the only significant building that now remains in Hove from before the Victorian period is the 13th-century church of St Andrew's. During the 19th century, Hove developed rapidly and by 1901 the population was 33,000. Due to the influence of the nearby Brunswick estate the streets were laid out in a neat grid system which has helped to produce the elegant town of today.

HOVE BRUNSWICK

The popularity of Brighton in the early 19th century led developers away from the town towards cheaper semi-rural sites where land was more readily available and local taxes less demanding. The Brunswick estate to the west of Brighton is the work of Charles Augustin Busby who went beyond mere overspill to produce a carefully planned Regency new town complete with all the necessary infrastructure for all the social groups who lived there.

SHOREHAM-BY-THE-SEA

Five miles west of Brighton and Hove is Shoreham-by-the-Sea. A settlement here is recorded in the Domesday Book and the town grew up around the 11th-century church of St Mary de Haura in an unusual grid pattern. The 12th-century building that now houses the Marlipins Museum is one of the oldest non-ecclesiastical buildings in the UK. Shoreham's natural harbour has provided a safe haven since Norman times but it was only in the 19th century when the railways arrived that the port was able to grow significantly. Several shipyards were established as well as a thriving coastal trade. Today, Shoreham operates as a mixed commercial port and cargoes include aggregates, sawn timber, steel, oil, locally-grown cereals and scrap metal. The harbour also houses yachts and fishing boats. The RNLI have maintained a lifeboat there since 1865.

SHOREHAM HARBOUR

A shingle beach runs along the south side of the spit that forms the harbour. At the head of the spit is an experimental fort built in 1857. Its main purpose was to try out the new rifle artillery and to see whether the fort could be used to withstand invasion. Decommissioned at the end of the 19th century, the barrack block was then used as a film studio. Shoreham Airport is the UK's oldest licensed airport and its Art Deco terminal is a listed building.

FINDON VILLAGE

The small village of Findon lies below the Neolithic flint mine and iron age fortress of Cissbury ring. The fort was used to defend the area against Saxon invaders but seems to have had very little effect in withstanding their attacks. Kings Aethelred II and Cnut established a royal mint at Cissbury and in 1866 a large hoard of Saxon coins was found in the area. Findon contains no fewer than 26 listed buildings including the church of St John the Baptist, parts of which date from the 11th century.

LANCING COLLEGE

Lancing College was founded in 1848 by Nathaniel Woodard. It is chiefly remarkable for its early French Gothic-style chapel. This was intended as a central minster for all the schools established by Woodard and is the largest school chapel in the world. It also has the largest rose window in England which is 32 feet (9m) in diameter and contains 30,000 separate pieces of glass. The college grounds extend to 550 acres.

HIGH SALVINGTON

The village of High Salvington, near Worthing, is the site of one of the country's few working post mills – where the building that houses the mill's machinery is mounted on a single post. This was built around 1750 and served the Worthing area until 1897. During much of the 20th century the mill was neglected although part of it was used as tea-room. A programme of restoration enabled the mill to begin grinding again in 1991.

WORTHING

For most of its history Worthing was a fishing and farming community (with the usual sideline of smuggling) but the rise of sea bathing gave the town new impetus from the 1790s onwards.

The 19th century saw Worthing expand rapidly though in a more haphazard manner than nearby Brighton, so there are fewer grand schemes or extensive terraces. Like Brighton the town benefited from royal patronage: in 1798, King George III sent his younger daughter Princess Amelia to Worthing in the hope that bathing in the sea would help her damaged knee. The king was clearly mindful that Amelia's elder brother the Prince Regent was in nearby Brighton and hoped that sending the young girl to a different town would keep her away from the influence of the dissolute prince and his entourage.

Oscar Wilde wrote *The Importance of Being Earnest* in Worthing in 1884 and its central character is named Ernest Worthing.

WORTHING PIER

The pier was built in 1861-2 and originally consisted of a 960ft (292m) promenade deck with a landing stage. The width of the end of the pier was increased to 105ft (32m) in 1888 and a 650-seat pavilion was added. The shoreward pavilion was built in 1926. Part of the pier was blown down in 1913 leaving the pavilion isolated and in 1933 a fire destroyed the original pavilion. Worthing pier is still operating in spite of these problems.

LITTLEHAMPTON

Originally known as Hampton this port on the mouth of the Arun was given the prefix "little" to distinguish it from Southampton. In the 16th century, Henry VIII's dockyards were located here and ship-building has continued ever since. Today, rather than constructing warships, Littlehampton is famous for yacht-building and a number of well-known boat-building companies have established themselves in the town.

AMBERLEY CASTLE *(left)*

The castle is built around a 12th-century manor house and village owned by the see of Chichester. The curtain walls and gatehouse were added in the mid 14th century. Ownership of the property passed to the crown after the dissolution of the monasteries and it remained in royal hands until 1749 when James Butler bought the castle for about £3,300. After his defeat at the battle of Worcester King Charles II stayed at Amberley on his way to Shoreham before he left for France. Restoration of the battlements began in 1893 but the castle was not opened to the public until 1989.

ARUNDEL

Taking its name from the river Arun, Arundel is an elegant town famous for both its castle and its cathedral. The castle was built at the end of the 11th century and extensively restored in the 19th century. It is the home of the Dukes of Norfolk. The Catholic cathedral at Arundel was commissioned by Henry, the 15th Duke of Norfolk, in December 1868. It was completed in 1873, to designs of Joseph Hansom, the inventor of the hansom cab. The cathedral is in the French Gothic-style and is built in brick with Bath stone cladding. In 1973 it was dedicated to the recently canonised St Philip Howard.

BOGNOR BUTLINS

Opened in 1960, the Bognor Regis Butlins is one of the three remaining holiday camps established by Billy Butlin. The others are at Minehead and Skegness. Famous for their "red coat" entertainment officers, Butlins holiday camps were a staple of British post-war holiday making. At the centre of the Bognor camp is the "Skyline Pavilion" which provides an all-weather focal point for activities.

FORD MARKET

This popular Sunday market takes place at Ford Airfield near Arundel and sells everything from household goods, car accessories, garden furniture to plants and local produce.

CHICHESTER MARINA

Chichester has the second largest marina in Britain. Set in an extensive natural harbour with 11 square miles of water it provides safe, sheltered boating in an area of outstanding natural beauty. The harbour straddles the Hampshire/West Sussex border and boasts 14 sailing clubs and 17 miles (27km) of channels around Chichester, Hayling and Southbourne. Beyond the Marina itself there are a host of other attractions such as the historic town of Chichester with its elegant cathedral or the Roman villa at Fishbourne.

SELSEY SANDBANKS

Selsey is a small town about 11 miles (17km) south of Chichester. It is the home of the astronomer Patrick Moore and saw the birth of the International Birdman Event (where contestants attempt to fly off the end of a pier) in 1971. Beyond the town lie the Selsey Sandbanks which are a well-known navigational hazard for ships in the area. The bank has been built up as a result of tides depositing sand in this area for many thousands of years.

SELSEY BILL

Selsey Bill is a low headland that stretches three miles out from the rest of the coastline. It is under constant attack from the tides of the English Channel and is protected by a variety of sea walls and other sea defences. Even a small rise in sea levels would make Selsey Bill disappear completely. There is a nature reserve at the northern end of the headland and the nearby saltmarsh provides a haven for over-wintering wildfowl.

CUCKMERE VALLEY

The Cuckmere Valley, near Seaford, attracts over 450,000 visitors a year. The beautiful river Cuckmere meanders through its lower valley and enters the sea next to the Seven Sisters cliffs. To the west of the river extensive water meadows form a maze of fresh water habitats that are popular with both local and transient wildlife. The Seven Sisters Country Park, to the east of the river, gives visitors access to a variety of natural habitats including saltmarsh, river meadows and the chalk grassland above the cliffs.

CUCKMERE HAVEN (right)

Cuckmere Haven is the only undeveloped river mouth on the South Coast; the haven's isolation made it a favoured spot for smuggling. The authorities tried to stop the practice but it was so widespread that they often failed. On two occasions in 1783, for instance, excise men were unable to intervene when gangs of 200 or 300 men openly carried away their contraband from Cuckmere Haven. Its shallow waters make a comfortable marine habitat for sealife and the area has been designated a Voluntary Marine Nature Reserve.

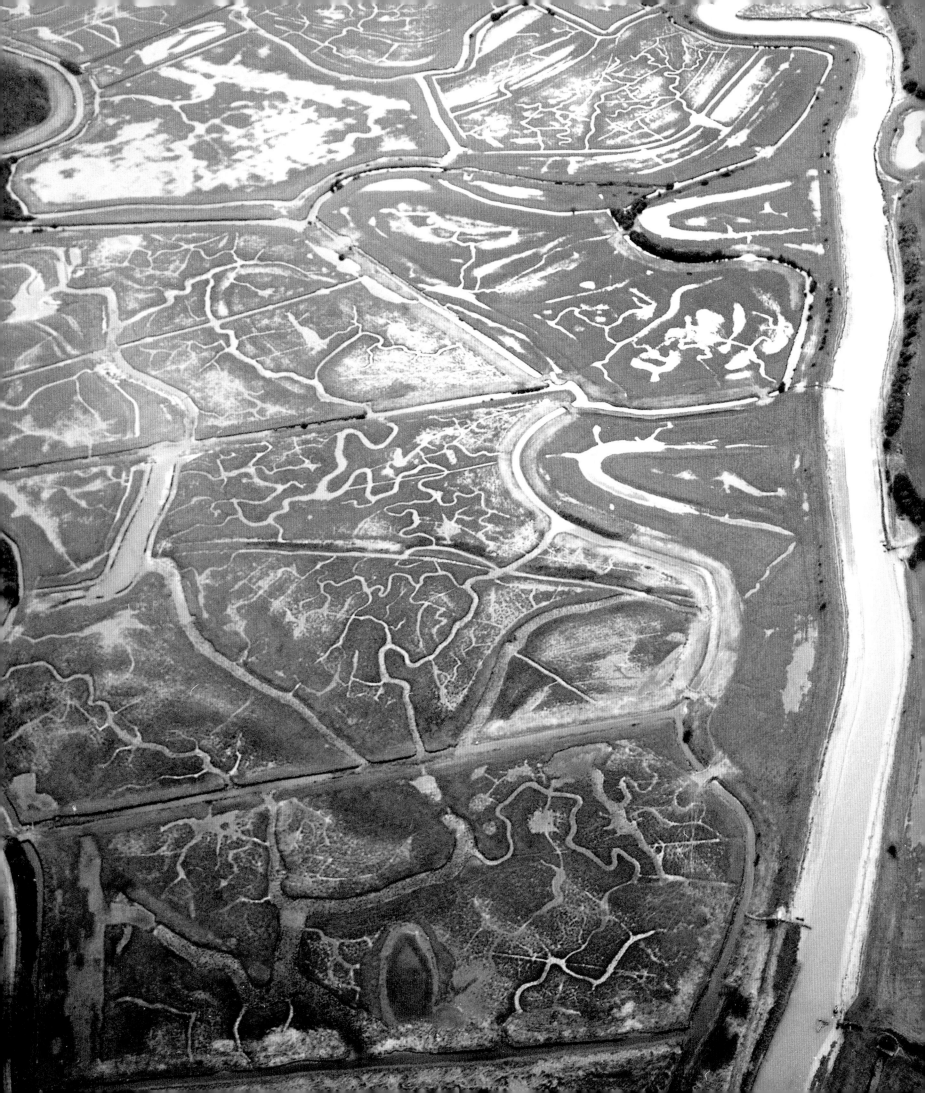

THE SEVEN SISTERS

The Seven Sisters chalk cliffs dramatically mark the point where the South Downs meet the sea. While all the cliffs have a look of permanency about them, in reality this section of the coast is being eroded away at an average rate of 30-40cm per year. The Sisters themselves are the peaks of the downland. Geologically the downs consist of a mixture of chalk and flint. As the sea erodes the cliffs away the flint is left behind to form the shingle of the beaches. This process can be observed at low tide when it is possible to walk from Cuckmere Haven to Beachy Head.

EASTBOURNE *(left)*

Eastbourne developed as a popular resort in the same period as Brighton; Brighton's prestige was the result of the presence of the Prince Regent whereas Eastbourne's began with the visit of four other children of King George III. Most of Eastbourne was owned by a few landowners such as the Duke of Devonshire and John Davies Gilbert. They sought to develop Eastbourne as a grand resort built "for gentlemen by gentlemen". Even today the front at Eastbourne is free of shops and retains an air of eminent Victorian respectability. The central feature of the Duke's development plan for the town was a wide tree-lined boulevard now known as Devonshire Place. In 1872 the promenade was built and the pier was opened. Meanwhile, the railway had arrived and the town's prosperity was assured well into the 20th century.

HASTINGS *(above)*

Hastings is deeply embedded in English consciousness as the site of the battle where William of Normandy defeated King Harold in 1066. But the town has an interesting history extending well beyond the battle. In the later middle ages Hastings was one of the prosperous Cinque Ports. When trade declined, fishing developed and it still boasts the largest beach-based fishing fleet in England. In the late 18th and 19th centuries Hastings benefited from the sea-bathing craze and became the favoured retreat of artists such as Dante Gabriel Rossetti and Holman Hunt who appreciated the town's coastal light and its clear air. Hastings is currently going through a period of regeneration. A new station has been opened and University Centre Hastings, an outpost of the University of Brighton, has been established.

BATTLE ABBEY

Battle Abbey is said to have been built by William the Conqueror in penance for the slaughter that took place at the Battle of Hastings; whether built in penance or celebration of his victory, the original abbey was a fine example of early Norman architecture. It was begun in 1076 but not consecrated until 1094, by which time William had been succeeded by his son William Rufus. It is said that the altar was built on the exact spot where King Harold was killed. The abbey was remodelled in the late 13th century but went into rapid decline after the dissolution of the monasteries. Little now remains of the abbey other than its ground plan and the remains of some of the ancillary buildings.

CAMBER SANDS

The extensive beaches at Camber Sands are as attractive to modern-day holiday-makers as they were to smugglers in the past. The area was once so notorious for smuggling that excise men built a watch house here in the early 1800s. The tower proved itself useful in 1821 when a gang of over 200 smugglers were spotted and a running battle ensued before the leading smuggler was captured. During the Second World War Camber Sands was used as a testing area for tanks.

BODIAM CASTLE

Work began on Bodiam Castle in 1385, which makes it a rather late example of Norman castle building – but a visually dramatic one nevertheless. The castle benefited from advances in contemporary castle building techniques and is centred on a courtyard rather than a fortified keep. It was also considerably more comfortable for its inhabitants than earlier castles. Bodiam was built in response to fears of a French invasion – an invasion that never came and the castle saw no significant military action even during the English Civil War.

HAYWARDS HEATH

Until the mid 19th century the land on which Haywards
Heath now stands was mostly given over to crop growing. In
1841 powerful landowners in the nearby village of Cuckfield
forced the route of the railway away from their land and
caused it to run through what is now Haywards Heath.
Growth followed rapidly as people found they could retreat
from London into the relative peace and calm of Sussex.
Cuckfield remains a small village but Haywards Heath
gained town status in 1862. At about the same time, the
county's asylum moved to Haywards Heath. The old asylum
building has recently been transformed into modern apart-
ments. Most of the substantial buildings in Haywards Heath
are Victorian and Edwardian, although in the 1930s
Franklands Village was set up to provide affordable housing.
In recent years the town has continued to prosper offering
work in the financial services sector and providing
commuter-belt housing for London.

HORSHAM

Horsham is the central town of Horsham district which has been an area of mixed farming and industry since Roman times. In the middle ages Horsham was an important market town and had its own assizes from the 14th century onwards. The iron industry provided wealth and prosperity for the north of the district, whilst the wool trade did the same for the south. By the end of the 16th century both of these activities had passed their peak and Horsham's population went into relative decline. Recent years have seen a reversal of this trend and Horsham is now a popular (and populous) location. The poet Percy Bysshe Shelley was born in Horsham, a fact that is commemorated by a large fountain in the town centre inspired by his poem *Mont Blanc*.

BALCOMBE VIADUCT

This dramatic structure stands just north of Haywards
Heath. The viaduct is a triumph of Victorian engineering
and was built in 1841 to cross the Ouse Valley. Balcombe
viaduct is around 1,500ft (457m) long; it has 37 arches and
was built using 11 million bricks specially imported from
Holland. It has recently been renovated and restored to
its original condition – although many locals claim that
the old viaduct looked far better than the renovated one!

HAMILTON PALACE

Hamilton Palace is a neo-classical building topped by a
copper dome. It is bigger than Buckingham Palace and
includes a 600ft (182m) art gallery. The walls of the
mausoleum are three feet thick and are designed to hold
the present owner's body for 5,000 years. It is estimated to
have cost £40m and is reportedly the most expensive
private house built in Britain for over a hundred years.

EAST SUSSEX GOLF CLUB

The East Sussex National Golf Club has two championship courses and has hosted the European Open twice. The west course is a par 72 and is 7,154 yards (6,541m) long. The east course runs to 7,138 yards (6,527m). Accommodation at the course is provided by the Horsted Place Country House Hotel. This Gothic-revival country house was built in 1850 for a wealthy merchant and much of the detail was designed by Augustus Pugin. The clubhouse complex provides tennis courts, a sauna, a solarium, an indoor swimming pool and conference facilities as well as the usual food, drink and shopping in very modern surroundings. The club also runs a golf academy.

HERSTMONCEUX

Herstmonceux Castle was the first brick-built castle in England. Construction started in 1441 and, from the outset, the focus was on the comfort and scale of the building rather than its defensive capabilities. The house prospered until after the Civil War but it was sold in 1700 and many of its bricks were used in the con-struction of Herstmonceux Place, further up the hill. Restoration began in the early 20th century. Herstmonceux Castle is also the site of the Royal Greenwich Observatory.

SURREY

STRETCHING FROM THE OUTSKIRTS OF LONDON in the north to Sussex in the south, Surrey contains elements of both traditional and modern which sit side by side and don't feel out of place. The North Downs and the spectacular Hog's Back are as rugged as they were in Anglo-Saxon times, whilst major urban centres like Woking, Camberley, Bagshot and Esher are still within easy reach of sites of outstanding natural beauty and elegant stately homes. Major traffic hubs such as the M25 and Gatwick Airport place Surrey firmly in the 21st century but many of its towns and villages still retain some of their centuries-old charm.

GATWICK AIRPORT

Gatwick is Britain's second busiest airport and more than 30m passengers pass through here each year. It has two terminals (North and South) and is well served by road and rail links to London and the south-east. Originally aimed at British and European destinations, aircraft from Gatwick now fly to destinations all round the world.

GATWICK AIRPORT M23/M25 INTERCHANGE

The M25 is London's outer ring road and the M23 carries traffic to and from Gatwick Airport. These two major arteries require vast amounts of space to provide a smooth traffic flow between them, although the shape of this interchange could also indicate a subtle patriotic intention on the part of its designers.

GROWTH OF GATWICK

Gatwick Airport began life in 1931 as a private airfield. It boasted a small terminal, a runway and some taxiways and aprons. Uniquely for the period, the airport had a direct subway and covered walkway link with the nearby railway station. The airfield grew substantially as an RAF base during the Second World War, even taking in a local racecourse, but by the end of the war the runway was still not properly paved. In 1953 Gatwick was designated as London's second airport after Heathrow. A three-year development programme transformed the old airfield into a modern facility with a 2,000ft

(609m) runway capable of landing the largest planes of the period. The terminal had by then expanded to include the railway station and featured the first covered walkway in the UK linking the terminal with the aircraft. Much of the traffic using the airport was domestic at first but as air travel became more popular in the 1970s and 80s Gatwick saw high volumes of charter flights and a steadily increasing number of scheduled international flights. The original terminals have been expanded and two more walkways have been built but Gatwick's popularity means that it is likely to expand even further.

EPSOM RACECOURSE

The potential of Epsom Downs as a horse-racing venue was first realised by Sir Charles Bunbury and Lord Derby. They saw that the unusual contours of the landscape would make a wonderful racecourse and in 1779 organised the first flat race on the site. It was called the Oaks after Lord Derby's estate. The Oaks, which was restricted to fillies, was soon followed by a race for horses for both sexes. The two men tossed a coin to decide on whose name would be used for the race and, as a result, the first Epsom Derby was run in 1780. The race has been run every June since then, even during the First and Second World Wars. In 1913 a suffragette named Emily Davison threw herself under King George V's horse and was killed. Other controversies that have surrounded the race have included the kidnapping of the popular Derby winner Shergar in 1983. The horse's whereabouts still remain a mystery.

BOX HILL

Box Hill is one of the summits of the North Downs.
It rises to a height of 634ft (193m) and has a 394ft (120m)
chalk cliff, which has been carved out by the river Mole.
The cliff is so steep that only yew and box trees can gain
a purchase in it, hence the name of the hill. Box Hill was
a popular tourist attraction even before the word
"tourist" was invented. The diarist John Evelyn and the
journalist Daniel Defoe both recorded comments about
the site and we have to assume that Jane Austen was a
visitor since she used a trip to Box Hill as a central
episode in *Emma*. The advent of the railways made
Box Hill a popular destination for Victorian Londoners.
In 1930 the television pioneer John Logie Baird
conducted some of his early experiments on Box Hill.
In 1912, 230 acres of Box Hill were purchased for the
nation and given to the National Trust. Since then the
estate has expanded to over 1,200 acres and in 1971 it was
declared an official Country Park. Box Hill is a habitat
for 40 out of the 58 British butterfly species.

DORKING *left*

Dorking owes its existence to a crossroads. The Roman Stane Street, connecting London to the south coast, crossed the east-west tracks of the North Downs at Dorking and, until the development of the railway, Dorking played an important role as a transport hub for walkers, riders and coaches. Dorking's pleasant situation and proximity to other beauty spots such as Box Hill and Cotmandene has always attracted visitors ranging from Jane Austen and Charles Dickens to EM Forster and John Keats. Daniel Defoe was educated in Dorking, Lawrence Olivier was born there and the composer Ralph Vaughan Williams spent most of his life in and around the town.

CATERHAM *(above)*

Caterham developed in two stages. Caterham on the Hill, the original settlement, is located close to Iron Age forts on a ridge of the North Downs. The fine Norman church of St Lawrence on the brow of the hill was built in 1095. The second settlement is Caterham Valley which began to develop in the Victorian period as prosperous Londoners, seeking escape from the city, built mansions along the Harestone Valley Road. The two parts of the town are connected by the steep Church Hill road. The sports car manufacturer Caterham Cars has its headquarters in the town — its most famous car, the Caterham Seven, has broken many UK and overseas records.

M25 MOTORWAY

The orbital motorway, the M25, which circles London, is approximately 121.5 miles (195km) in circumference and runs across the top of Surrey. Along with the Great Wall of China it is said to be one of the few man-made objects visible from near Earth orbit. It is believed to be Europe's busiest motorway and is currently used by over 200,000 vehicles every day. Construction of what is now known as the M25 began in 1957 with the opening of the Dartford Tunnel approaches but the full London Orbital scheme was not approved until 1975. The final section was opened in 1986. Plans are in hand to expand the width of the motorway along most of its length. The official archive for the history of the M25 is located in Surrey.

HICKSTEAD (right)

Hickstead is the home of the All England Jumping Course. This was created in 1960 by Douglas Bunn on land surrounding Hickstead Place. His intention was to provide the United Kingdom with a show-jumping course that was on a par with the best facilities in the United States and Europe. Hickstead hosts the British Nations Cup and Grand Prix and has been the venue for many national and international competitions. The showground has six arenas, permanent seating for over 5,000 spectators and 26 corporate hospitality suites as well as many other facilities.

CRANLEIGH SCHOOL

Cranleigh School was founded in
1865 as a boys' boarding school and
occupies a 200-acre site. The buildings,
mainly in brick, range from Gothic
and neo-Palladian through to the ultra-
modern sports centre. Girls were
admitted to the sixth form in the early
1970s and the school, which houses
over 600 pupils, is now fully co-
educational.

DUNSFOLD AERODROME

Dunsfold Aerodrome near Godalming
was a Second World War fighter base.
After the war British Aerospace used
the aerodrome to test aircraft such as
the Harrier Jump Jet and the Hawk
trainer. British Aerospace withdrew
from Dunsfold in 2002. Today the BBC
motoring programme *Top Gear* is
recorded on the site.

SURREY WEALTH

In the early 20th century Surrey became known as the "stockbroker belt" – a place where affluent City workers lived in mock-Tudor mansions, played golf at the weekend and drove around in Bentleys and Jags. Today's Surrey commuter is a far cry from this image but the large houses and the affluence still remains. Now the county has a reputation as a place where pop stars, media celebrities and sports superstars choose to live, attracted by the large secluded houses and excellent transport links.

HAMPSHIRE

THE COUNTY OF HAMPSHIRE contains some of Britain's most historic locations, including Winchester, the county town and formerly the capital of the Saxon kingdom of Wessex. To the west lies the New Forest which was created by William the Conqueror as a hunting reserve and to the south, the ports of Southampton and Portsmouth. There is also a strong military connection in towns such as Portsmouth, Aldershot and Farnborough indicating the county's strategic importance. Hampshire has a great deal to offer tourists: those with a literary inclination can visit Jane Austen's or Charles Dickens' birthplaces; the more mechanically minded can investigate motor cars at Beaulieu, submarines in Gosport or aircraft at Farnborough; those in search of the countryside can visit the New Forest, walk the South Downs Way or explore the glorious coastline.

NAVY SHIPS

The history of Great Britain is punctuated with naval achievements and ships based in Portsmouth were at the heart of many important maritime battles. The defeat of the Spanish Armada in 1588, the battle of Trafalgar in 1805 and, during the Second World War, the battle of the Atlantic were all engagements won as a result of Portsmouth's seafaring tradition. There has been a strong naval presence in the town since King Richard I decided to set up a permanent naval base there in 1198 and the first docks were built 12 years later.

GOSPORT, PORTSMOUTH AND HAYLING ISLAND

The city of Portsmouth is largely built on Portsea Island at the confluence of the Solent and the English Channel.
To the west (foreground of the picture) lies Gosport and to the east is Hayling Island. The main Portsmouth harbour
is to the west of the city and the large sheltered bay known as Langstone Harbour is to the east. A regular ferry service
runs between Portsmouth and its sister town of Gosport. Hayling Island is a popular holiday resort and the area
around is reputed to provide some of the best windsurfing in the country.

HAYLING ISLAND

Hayling Island is roughly triangular in shape and is bounded to the east by Chichester Harbour and to the west by Langstone Harbour. To the south is the Solent. Hayling has over three miles of beaches. Its sheltered waters provide an ideal location for watersports of all kinds; windsurfing was invented on Hayling Island and Hayling is an international venue for the sport.

SOUTH HAYLING

Beyond the village of South Hayling is the south-eastern tip of the island known as Sandy Point. This area of sandy heathland is largely unspoiled and has been designated as a nature reserve. It provides a habitat for several important species of plants and bird.

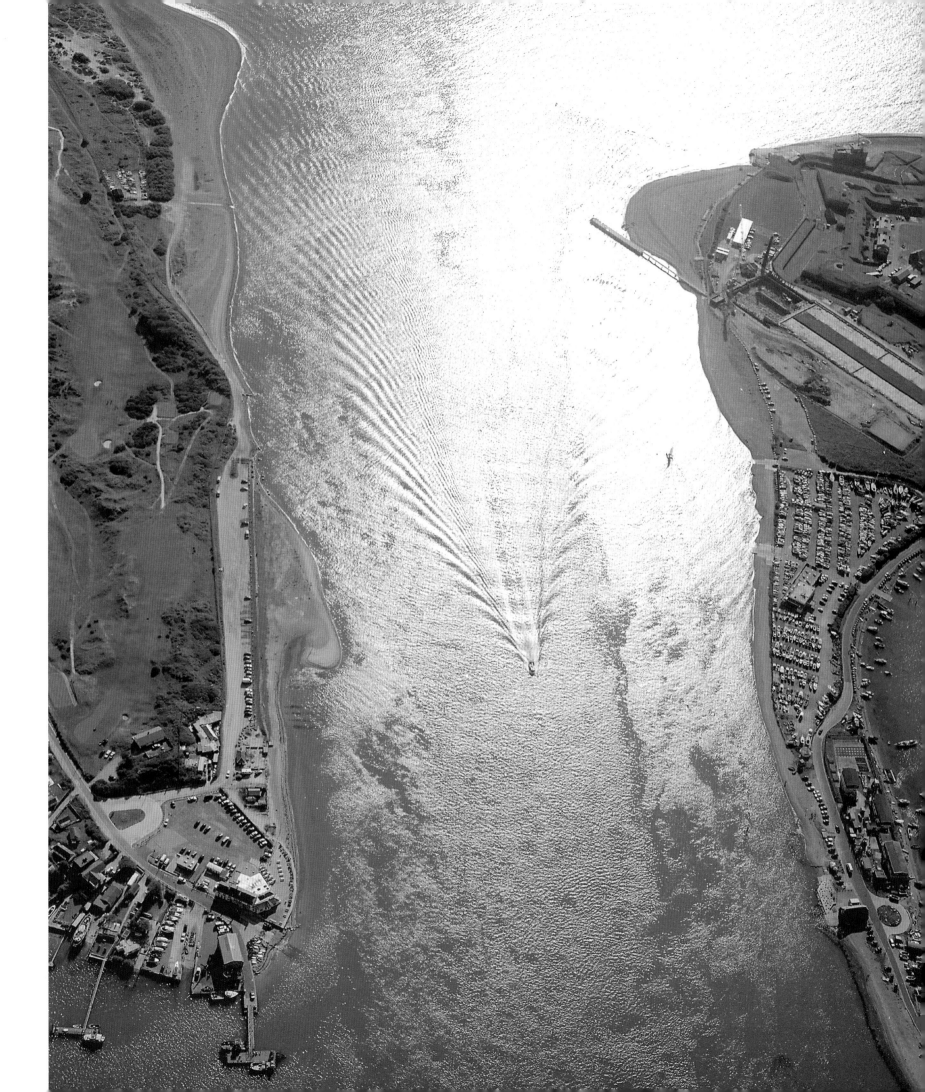

PORTSMOUTH

Although Old Portsmouth became a naval base in 1200, it took 200 years for serious defences to be placed around the port. In 1418 King Henry V ordered a wooden round tower to be built at the mouth of the harbour. Henry VIII had the round tower rebuilt in stone and also added Southsea Castle to the town's defences. At about the same time the world's first dry dock was built at Porstmouth. Further

improvements to Portsmouth's fortifications were funded by England's first official state lottery. At the height of Portmouth's role as a naval dock in 1800, the port accommodated 684 Royal Navy ships and was the world's largest industrial complex. During the Second World War the town suffered heavy bombing and many of its original buildings have disappeared or have been extensively rebuilt.

SOUTHSEA

The suburb of Southsea began to develop at the beginning of the 19th century and initially provided housing for some of the skilled workers of Portsmouth. Expansion continued and Southsea's beach became a holiday resort. The stony beach has two piers and is the location of the D-Day Museum. The large distance between the beach and the first buildings was designed so that troops could muster on the foreshore. Southsea Castle was the spot from which Henry VIII watched the Mary Rose sink in 1545.

SPINNAKER TOWER

The Spinnaker Tower rises 558ft (170m) from the sea next to the Gunwharf Quay development – two and a half times the height of Nelson's Column in London. When it is completed in 2005 it will be the tallest public viewing tower in the UK. The tower is sponsored by the Millennium Commission and its estimated cost is £25m. It is intended to be the centrepiece of the regeneration of Old Portsmouth harbour and to provide a new coastal landmark that will be instantly recognisable to anyone approaching the port.

GUNWHARF QUAYS *(right)*

Built on the site of Royal Navy ordnance yards, Gunwharf Quays was opened to the public in 2001. It is a shopping and entertainment complex that houses a casino, a bowling alley, a multi-screen cinema and even a comedy club amongst its collection of shops, restaurants, bars and hotels. It is another aspect of the drive to regenerate the older areas of Portsmouth.

THE NAVAL DOCKYARDS

The dockyards began their first major expansion when Charles II created the Royal Navy and made the dock the Royal Dockyard. By 1802 the dockyard had become the world's largest manufactory. The dockyards produced the world's first steam screw warship in 1829 and the first major oil-powered warship in 1913. *HMS Andromeda*, launched in 1967, was the last of 286 ships built in Portsmouth. The naval base remains the home port of the Royal Navy and it maintains numerous aircraft carriers, assault ships and destroyers.

HMS VICTORY (right)

HMS Victory was the flagship of Vice Admiral Horatio Nelson at the battle of Trafalgar on October 21 1805. Nelson's victory on that day effectively crushed French naval power for a generation. However, Nelson, resplendent in his medals and ribbons, caught the attention of a French sharpshooter and did not survive the battle. *HMS Victory*, which carried over a hundred guns and had a crew of 800 men, is now on permanent display in the Portsmouth docks along with two other famous ships, the *Mary Rose* and *HMS Warrior*.

No Man's Land Fort (right)

One of four "Palmerston" forts designed to defend the approaches to Portsmouth, No Man's Land Fort was constructed between 1864 and 1880. It is essentially a gun platform on several levels. The other forts are St Helen's, Horse Sand and Spitbank. None of the four were ever used in anger – apart possibly from the filming of a famous *Dr Who* episode. No Man's Land Fort has its own lighthouse and can be accessed by boat or helicopter. It is also licensed for weddings.

SOUTHSEA MARINA

Southsea Marina is located in a sheltered site on the Rastney peninsula, the most easterly point of Portsea island. It is convenient for access to Langstone harbour and the rest of the Solent. An automatic tidal flap gate allows unrestricted movement in and out of the Marina for around three hours on either side of high water. Facilities at the Marina include a boatyard as well as shops, bars and restaurants.

PORTSMOUTH FC

"Pompey", as Portsmouth FC is known to its supporters, was founded in 1898. The team has won the Football League Championship twice and made three appearances in the FA Cup final, although they have won it only once. They play at Fratton Park which has a capacity of approximately 20,200 and still has a traditional uncovered "away" end.

PORT SOLENT MARINA

Port Solent Marina is situated within Portsmouth Harbour; alongside the marine facilities it has a cinema and a health and fitness club as well as a wide variety of shops and restaurants. A sailing school also operates from the Marina and provides courses at every level from novice to coastal skipper.

THE SOLENT

The Solent separates the Isle of Wight from the mainland; it was formed from a drowned river valley at the end of the last ice age. Because tides flow in at each end of the island, tidal patterns in the area are very complex. The Solent gives access to the ports of Southampton and Portsmouth and has been considered to be of great strategic importance since the middle ages. Henry VIII built fortifications at either end of the waterway and these were added to in the 19th century. The combination of scenic beauty, historical interest and challenging sailing makes the Solent an extremely popular yachting centre. A cricket match is played once a year in the middle of the Solent when Bramble Bank emerges from the sea during the lowest tide of the year. Members of two sailing clubs race out to the bank, set up stumps and an impromptu public house, and play until the pitch submerges.

FERRIES

Ferries are a very common sight on the Solent. Up to five companies operate ferries to the Isle of Wight and three large companies operate ferries to the Continent and to the Channel Islands. Over 8m passengers travel to the Isle of Wight every year.

HAMBLE-LE-RICE

The sheltered waters near Hamble-le-Rice, where the river Hamble flows into Southampton Water, are very popular with yacht sailors. An aircraft factory in the village is testimony to the area's long association with aviation. The first Englishman to fly, AV Roe, built the original factory there and many early aviatiors, including Amy Johnson, were associated with it. During World War II Hamble-le-Rice was a base for the repair and service of Spitfires and Hurricanes. These were returned to RAF airfields by a team of female pilots.

ROYAL VICTORIA COUNTRY PARK

The Royal Victoria Country Park is the site of the UK's first purpose-built military hospital. Its layout was designed according to principles established by Florence Nightingale. Fans of Sherlock Holmes will know that this is where Dr Watson served as an army doctor. Most of the hospital was burned down in the 1960s but there is an exhibition of its history in the Chapel.

SOUTHAMPTON WATER

Southampton Water is a drowned river valley that formed when the glaciers receded about 10,000 years ago. The rivers Test, Itchen and Hamble flow into it and the city of Southampton is at its northern end. To the west is the New Forest. The water is a vital seaway for the city of Southampton and it has been progressively deepened by dredging over the years as ships have grown bigger.

SUPERLINERS

The P&O cruise ship the *Oriana* in dock at Southampton. The port has long been a base for cruise holidays. The boat is 853ft (260m) and can accommodate 2,273 passengers in its 914 cabins.

FORD SWAYTHLING PLANT

The Ford Motor Company employs approximately 1,750 staff and produces between 60-70,000 vehicles a year at its transit van production factory in the Swaythling district of northern Southampton. In operation since the 1970s, the plant has built over half of all the Ford transits in the world – a total of well over 1.5m units. The plant was re-equipped in 1986 and uses 125 robots in the production process.

VEHICLES FOR EXPORT

Southampton is the UK's leading port for the import and export of vehicles. Almost one-third of the production at the Ford plant is exported, mostly to other European markets. Ford's location in Southampton gives it easy access to both sea and road-based transport.

SOUTHAMPTON DOCKS

Although Southampton has been a port since Roman times it did not acquire its first dock until 1836. The combination of the dock with rail transport ensured that the port boomed and by 1936 Southampton docks handled 46% of all the United Kingdom's ocean-going passenger traffic. In that year 18.7m tonnes of shipping operated by 32 separate companies used Southampton to serve 160 ports worldwide. In the 19th century all ships would have been loaded and unloaded by hand. Most modern cargoes are transported in containers which can be easily off-loaded and transferred to goods trains or lorries.

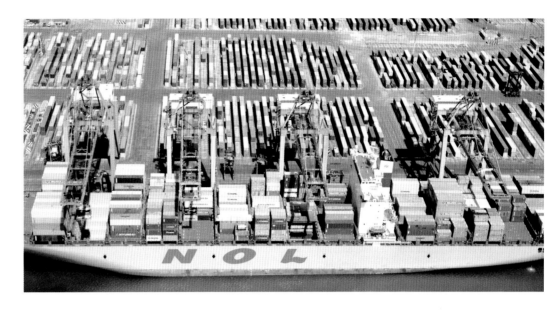

THE *QE2* AT ANCHOR

Southampton is probably most famous for its association with the transatlantic passenger trade. With the invention of steam and the growing prosperity of the United States, a luxury transatlantic run became possible and popular towards the end of the 19th century. Great shipping lines such as Cunard (based in Liverpool) and the White Star Line competed to achieve the fastest and most luxurious crossings. The White Star Line, which built the *Titanic*, began operating from Southampton in 1907. Today only the *QE2* provides a regular transatlantic service during the summer months.

FAWLEY OIL REFINERY *(right)*

Esso's Fawley oil refinery was opened in 1951 by the then Prime Minister Clement Atlee and is the largest oil refinery in the United Kingdom. It employs around 1,400 staff and handles 22m tonnes of crude oil every year. The refinery processes an average of 300,000 barrels of crude oil every day and it supplies over 15% of the United Kingdom's oil products. The majority of the oil currently comes from the North Sea but the refinery also imports oil from the Middle East and Russia. The jetty at the terminal is about a mile long and can handle over 2,000 ship movements a year.

St Mary's Southampton FC

Southampton FC was formed in 1885 and was originally known as Southampton St Mary's FC. Nicknamed "the Saints", in 1898 they moved to a newly-built ground called the Dell and played there for the next 103 years. In 2001 the club moved again – to the new St Mary's stadium. Built at a cost of £32m this all-seater stadium has a capacity of 32,000 and features two large screens, one above each goal, where fans can see replays of match action, half-time scores and other information. The stadium is noted for its friendly stewards and operates a strict no-smoking policy within the ground.

RIVER BEAULIEU
(left)

The River Beaulieu runs into the Solent almost opposite Cowes on the Isle of Wight. The wide stretch of water at the head of the valley provides extensive sailing and sheltered harbours. About halfway down the open stretch of water is the 18th-century shipbuilding village of Buckler's Hard. Founded by the Montagu family in 1724 the village used local oak trees to build ships for Nelson's fleet. The oak woodlands still surround the village which preserves much of the atmosphere of its shipbuilding days. Near the village there is a yacht harbour that provides berths for 110 boats.

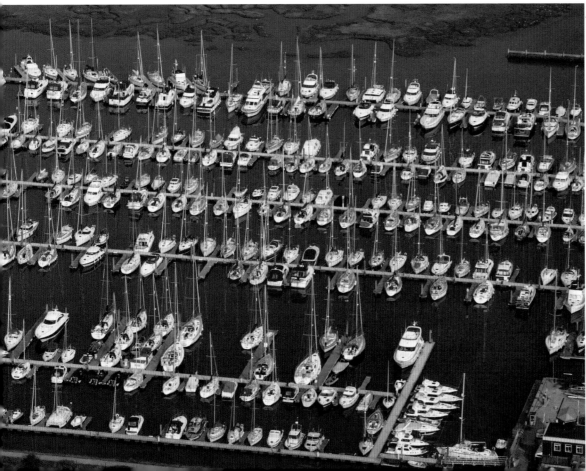

LYMINGTON *(above and left)*

Lymington is a small port on the Solent situated across from Yarmouth on the Isle of Wight. A ferry service runs between the two towns. In common with many towns on the South Coast Lymington developed during the Georgian era and it still preserves many aspects of that period; some streets and even the dock are still cobbled. There are salt marshes on either side of the estuary from which the town used to produce salt. Another early industry was smuggling. Today Lymington is a major yachting centre. There are two marinas close to the town and it is also possible to moor in the town itself at the town quay.

ISLE OF WIGHT

THE ISLE OF WIGHT IS A ROUGHLY DIAMOND-SHAPED ISLAND off the southern coast of England opposite Portsmouth and Southampton. The island has had a turbulent history because of its proximity to the mainland and over the years has been raided or conquered by British, Roman, Jute, Saxon, Danish, Norman and French forces. The Norman castle at Carisbrooke was for a long time the island's only defence but as the Solent became more important for the English navy more land-based fortifications were added, starting in the reign of Henry VIII. It is doubtful whether Charles I was fond of the Isle of Wight as he was imprisoned at Carisbrooke after his defeat in the Civil War but it was certainly a hit with Queen Victoria. She built her summer retreat at Osborne and triggered the island's transformation into a fashionable Victorian resort.

ISLE OF WIGHT FERRIES
Most passenger traffic to the Isle of Wight is by traditional ferry and high-speed catamarans. Ferry ports on the island include Cowes, East Cowes, Fishbourne, Ryde and Yarmouth. On the mainland, ferries start at Southampton, Portsmouth, Lymington and Southsea. The cost of taking a car to the island is quite high, whilst going as a foot passenger is relatively cheap. This price difference has discouraged car travel from the mainland and has helped the island to remain relatively unspoiled.

THE NEEDLES
Situated on the extreme western end of the Isle of Wight, the Needles are part of the same geological formation that gives rise to the South Coast, the White Cliffs of Dover, the Seven Sisters and Beachy Head.

COWES WEEK

Yachting became fashionable in the early 19th century and there have been regattas on the Isle of Wight since 1812. The regatta at Cowes has been held every year (apart from the two world wars) since 1826. It quickly gained royal approval and attendance at Cowes became part of the social calendar for the upper classes. Cowes week (currently lasting eight days) is traditionally held on the Saturday after the last Tuesday in July and attracts competitors from all over the world.

ROUND THE ISLAND RACE

This race starts and concludes Cowes Week and was first sailed in 1931. It attracts yachts of all classes and around 1,500 boats compete, from giant catamarans to simple cruising yachts. The fastest can circumnavigate the island in around four hours but some sail right up to the race's 14-hour time limit. Yachts compete against other vessels in their class and the overall winner is presented with the Gold Roman Bowl – one of the most coveted prizes in yachting.

COWES

Cowes and East Cowes are situated on the opposite banks of the river Medina. The two settlements owe their names to "cowforts" or "cowes", small forts set up by Henry VIII to defend the island from attack. The West Cowes fort eventually became the home of the Royal Yacht Squadron but the eastern fort has long disappeared. The town became a world-renowned centre for yachting after the Royal Yacht Squadron began organising regattas from 1826 onwards. East Cowes is the location of Queen Victoria's retreat at Osborne. Cowes is a popular sailing port all year round but during Cowes Week the town's population more than doubles as tourists and competitors flock to watch events such as the Admiral's Cup.

UNDER SAIL

Sailing historic ships, some restored and some replicas, is now a popular pastime, celebrated in such events as the Cutty Sark Tall Ships Race and the Parade of Sail. Some tall ships can be booked for holidays whilst many are used by youth-orientated charities for training and team-building.

SONIA

On September 1 1999 the *MV Sonia* had just left Southampton en route for Greece when water was discovered in the engine room. The vessel anchored in Sandown Bay and attempts at repairs were begun. Unfortunately sea-water continued to flow into the ship and there was a risk that 447 tonnes of fuel oil might be released into the bay. The vessel's owners were reluctant to deal with the problem and local salvage crews and equipment had to be called in to return *Sonia* to Southampton.

RYDE

Ryde is the largest town on the Isle of Wight and developed during the Victorian period as a seaside resort. Its pier was the first to be built (in 1814) and is the second longest in Britain at 2,250ft (685m). Unlike most piers it still serves as a dock for ferry services partly because of the great width of Ryde Sands at low tide. The First Fleet (the first 11 ships to carry convicts to Australia) anchored off the Mother Bank, just offshore from Ryde, before setting sail for Botany Bay in 1787; significantly, there is now a city of Ryde near Sydney Australia.

SANDOWN BAY

Sandown, on the south-east coast of the Isle of Wight, shares Sandown Bay with the town of Shanklin further south. Both towns are famous for their miles of sandy beaches. The town features broad promenades and public gardens as well as a fine selection of mid-to-late Victorian villas and townhouses. Also dating from the period are a Palmerston fort and a pier. The fort now houses a zoo. Sandown is connected to Ryde and Shanklin by rail on what is possibly the shortest commercial rail network (8.5miles/13km) in the UK.

SANDOWN BEACH

Within easy reach of Sandown are a wide variety of areas of natural and scientific interest. North of the town lies Culver Down, a typical chalk downland habitat which is popular with the many seabirds that nest on the nearby cliffs. Inland from the town are the Sandown Levels, which are freshwater wetlands that provide excellent birdwatching opportunities. Also within easy reach is Borthwood, an appealing woodland area. The sea area in front of Sandown is a special Area of Conservation for the beaches, local reefs and sea bed. When the tide is very low a petrified forest can be seen in the northern part of Sandown Bay; fragments of petrified wood are often washed up on the beach.

SANDOWN PIER

Construction of Sandown Pier began in 1876 and the pier was opened to the public in 1879. The first pier was rather short at 360ft (109m) and so an extension was built in 1895 which took the pier to a more impressive 875ft (266m). The advantage of the extended pier was that it provided better docking facilities at all states of the tide. A 1,000-seat pavilion was added at the shoreward end of the pier in 1933 and the pavilion at the pier head was converted for use as a ballroom at the same time. The pier head was remodelled in 1954 and the pier head pavilion was demolished in 1968. The refurbished shoreward pavilion now houses a theatre as well as amusement arcades, cafes and restaurants.

SHANKLIN *(left)*

The town owes its growth to the beaches of Sandown Bay, the presence of a medicinal spring and the deeply cut chalk valley known as the Chine. In the early 19th century it was a rural retreat where rooms could be let in summer but the arrival of the railway in 1864 made the town into a fashionable Victorian watering hole. A pier was built in 1890 (unfortunately this was washed away by storms in 1987) followed by a cliff lift in 1892; this linked the main town with the undercliff esplanade. During the Second World War oil was pumped from Shanklin to France as part of the PLUTO (Pipe Line Under The Ocean) project. Modern Shanklin maintains much of its Victorian charm and the 45ft (13m) waterfall of the Chine is as dramatic as ever.

VENTNOR *(above)*

In the early 19th century Ventnor consisted of two farms, a mill, and some fishing shacks. The area was isolated from the rest of the island by the high downs and poor roads. By 1830 it had a population of 77 but in that year the physician Sir James Clarke declared that Ventnor's climate was ideal for the treatment of pulmonary disease. Ventnor quickly became established as a health resort and in 1867 the Royal National Hospital for Consumption and Diseases of the Chest was founded with 155 beds. The railways arrived in Ventnor in 1866 and by 1888 a regular packet steamer service ran during the summer. Now thoroughly connected to the modern world, Ventnor reached its peak as a resort in the Edwardian period just prior to the First World War.

VENTNOR CLIFFS

Ventnor's mild climate is fully exploited at the Ventnor Botanic Gardens which now occupy the site of the Royal National Hospital for Diseases of the Chest. There are 22 acres of gardens and a temperate house which houses more exotic plants. Ventnor's western esplanade has a part sand, part fine shingle beach which makes it ideal for sunbathing and swimming whilst the newly opened Ventnor Haven provides excellent sailing facilities. Nearby is Bonchurch where Charles Dickens wrote part of *David Copperfield*.

CARISBROOKE CASTLE

The Isle of Wight's low-lying position and many convenient landing places made it peculiarly vulnerable to attack. It is therefore rather surprising to find the island's only significant castle so far inland. It was built in the 11th century but was frequently modified to cope with threats from invaders – usually the French. In the early 12th century a polygonal keep and stone curtain walls were added to the original "motte and bailey", and the twin-towered gatehouse was constructed at the end of the 14th century. Finally, the medieval castle was enclosed by long, straight walls and arrowhead bastions as a defence against Spanish artillery in the 1590s. The castle has a fine 13th-century chapel. King Charles I fled to Carisbrooke in November 1647 and was kept there as a prisoner until September 1648. The rooms he occupied are now a museum.

ST CATHERINE'S POINT *(left)*

St Catherine's Point is the southernmost tip of the Isle of Wight. This part of the coast is highly susceptible to erosion and approximately 900ft (274m) of the southern coastal area has been lost to the sea in the last 50 years. The frequent landslips have created the Undercliff, a wide coastal terrace that runs between Ventnor and St Catherine's Point. Just inland from St Catherine's Point is St Catherine's Hill, the highest point on the Isle of Wight at 780ft (237m). On top of the hill, in the form of an unusual octagonal tower, is the second-oldest lighthouse in Britain. This was built as a penance when some local landowners "liberated" the wine from a wrecked ship. The wine belonged to a monastery and the Pope ordered the landowners to build a lighthouse tower and an oratory in compensation. The oratory has almost completely disappeared but the tower can still be visited.

FRESHWATER BAY *(above, and above right)*

Freshwater Bay sweeps gently towards the westerly tip of the Isle of Wight. The town has a small beach and is an excellent starting point for walking along the cliffs that dominate most of the bay. The Tennyson Trail to the Needles starts here. The pioneering Victorian photographer Julia Margaret Cameron lived at Dimbola Lodge, Freshwater Bay where she photographed some of the cream of Victorian society.

ALUM BAY *(left)*

The strata in this area run vertically rather than horizontally and have been exposed by the steep limestone valley of Alum Bay Chine. The mixture of red, green, grey and white rocks is very interesting. Beach access is via a flight of 188 steps or a chairlift.

THE NEEDLES *(right)*

The Needles are named after a slender tapering pinnacle that was washed into the sea in 1764. The large gap in the current line of rocks marks its location and its stump can be seen at low tide when it forms a dangerous reef. The missing needle was about 120ft (36m) high whilst the highest of the remaining Needles rise to a height of approximately 100ft (30m).

NEEDLES LIGHTHOUSE

A lighthouse was built on the headland above the Needles in 1785 but at 462ft (140m) above sea level it was generally considered to be too high. A replacement was built in 1859 on the base of the most westerly rock. The light is 80ft (24m) above the high water mark and can be seen from 14 miles (22km) away at sea level.

TOTLAND

Totland Bay faces north towards the mainland and is well positioned for viewing shipping. Near the village is the spot where Marconi broadcast the first-ever radio signal. The mast from which he sent a message to a ship at sea on November 6 1897 no longer exists but a granite memorial marks the place where it stood.

YARMOUTH

Yarmouth is a yachting and ferry port on the western side of the Isle of Wight. A ferry service from Yarmouth to Lymington was inaugurated in 1830. The journey time of about 30 minutes has not changed significantly since. The village acquired a pier, mainly to allow ferries to dock, in 1876. Modern Yarmouth remains very much a yachting and fishing base and it is the easiest access point for such attractions as Alum Bay and the Needles.

DORSET

THE SOFT CHALK of the eastern part of the south coast gives way to much tougher limestone in Dorset. The wind, sea and rain have to work much harder to carve the coastal rocks but in doing so they have created some spectacular landscapes. By the time of the Norman Conquest, Dorset had settled down to a pattern of agriculture that remained stable until the beginning of the last century. Life in 19th-century Dorset has been made familiar by the works of Thomas Hardy whose fictional "Wessex" was closely based on his native Dorset. Another 19th-century figure who has played a role in shaping the 21st century county is Mary Anning whose skill as a fossil-hunter first drew attention to the wealth of fossils near Lyme Regis. The Dorset coast, from the Old Harry rocks westward, is now part of the Jurassic Coast World Heritage site.

OLD HARRY ROCKS

The Old Harry Rocks, near Swanage, are a group of eroded chalk features that include islands, stacks, stumps, caves and a natural arch. They mark the point where the Purbeck Hills fall into the sea and are the eastern limit of the Jurassic Coast World Heritage site. Old Harry has been around for about 200 years but the rock known as Old Harry's Wife collapsed about 50 years ago and can now only be seen as a stump at low tide.

Christchurch

The natural sheltered harbour at Christchurch has made it an important port since the Iron Age. The rivers Avon and the Stour both enter the sea here and in Saxon times the settlement was called "Tweoxneam" or "Twynham" meaning "place between two rivers". The modern name of Christchurch derives from the priory church which still dominates the town's skyline. Building work on the church started in 1094 but additions and modifications continued throughout the medieval period. Christchurch also had a Norman Castle but this did not survive the Civil War. In the 18th century smuggling was common in the area around Christchurch: on July 15 1784 a full-blown battle between smugglers and excise men erupted at Mudeford. Now a centre for fishing, yachting and other water-related activities, Christchurch is part of a continuous conurbation with Bournemouth and Poole.

BOURNEMOUTH

Bournemouth owes its rapid growth to its favourable climate and the Victorian fondness for sea-bathing. Wealthy invalids (including Prime Minister Disraeli who went there for his gout) flocked to the town and brought about a period of unprecedented prosperity. The town's glass-roofed winter gardens hosted concerts conducted by Elgar, Sibelius and Holst and the luxurious Mont Dore Hotel boasted one of the first telephones in England; its number was simply "3". Bournemouth was not very lucky with its piers, however. The first pier, built in 1856, was simply a short wooden jetty. This was replaced in 1871 but the wooden supports were attacked by worms and had to be replaced by cast iron. Despite this stronger structure, the landing stage was swept away in 1867 and further storm damage occurred in 1876. Finally, a new (and long-lasting) pier was constructed in 1880.

SANDBANKS *(below)*

Stretching out over the mouth of Poole harbour is the small peninsula known as Sandbanks. Its 3 miles (5km) of well-kept, fine sandy beach are extremely popular with holidaymakers and it has been awarded the prestigious European Union Blue Flag environmental award for a record 14 years in a row. Behind the beaches there was once a shanty town of converted railway carriages and sheds used as summer dwellings but the last of these disappeared in the 1960s. Sandbanks is now one of the most sought after beach areas in the country. The main road down the peninsula is known as "millionaires' row" and competition for house plots in the single square

kilometre available has meant that Sandbanks has the third highest land value by area in the world. A chain ferry connects Sandbanks to Studland across the mouth of Poole Harbour.

POOLE HARBOUR *(right)*

Poole boasts the world's second largest natural harbour after Sydney in Australia. Its extensive sheltered waters cover 22 square miles (36 sq km) and provide a magnificent location for sailing and extensive mudflats and marshland which are of great importance for feeding and roosting birds. The harbour also houses a busy ferry terminal running boats to the Channel Islands and France.

WEYMOUTH

Weymouth has been a port since Roman times and even today maintains a healthy level of business with the Continent and the Channel Islands. As well as its harbour Weymouth has a long sandy beach that has been attracting holidaymakers since 1789 when King George III went there to recover from an attack of porphyria. It was believed that sea bathing would be good for his health and the king entered the sea from a newly invented bathing machine. When he emerged a band played "God Save the King". George eventually bought a house at Weymouth and much of the architecture on today's seafront is Georgian in origin. A less happy connection for Weymouth is the fact that it is thought to be the place where the Black Death arrived in England, carried by rats aboard a visiting spice ship in 1348.

WEYMOUTH WHITE HORSE

King George III's visits to Weymouth brought great prosperity to the town and local people showed their appreciation by carving an equestrian image of him on a nearby hillside. The king is said to have been dismayed by the fact that it showed him riding away from Weymouth but by 1808, when the chalk figure of a white horse and its rider is known to have been completed, George's health had deteriorated so much that he never returned.

PORTLAND AND PORTLAND BILL

Portland is an island off the coast near Weymouth. It is approximately four miles (6km) long and one and a half miles (2.4km) wide and is connected to the mainland by Chesil Beach. Portland Bill is the southern tip of the island and is famous for its lighthouse. The current lighthouse was built in 1903 and is 135ft (41m) tall. Portland is composed mainly of limestone and Portland stone has long been valued for its durability as a building material. Christopher Wren chose it for St Paul's Cathedral and it is estimated that 6m tons of Portland stone were used to rebuild London after the Great Fire of 1666. Other buildings that have used Portland stone include the Victoria and Albert Museum, New Scotland Yard and the United Nations headquarters in New York. One of Portland's disused quarries is now a sculpture park. Portland harbour has an area of 2,130 acres (862ha) and is one of the largest harbours in the world. Many units of the Royal Navy were stationed there during the Second World War and as result the island was heavily bombed.

CHESIL BEACH *(above)*

The technical term for Chesil Beach is a "tombolo" meaning a beach or bar that connects two pieces of land together. At 18 miles (28km) Chesil Bank is the longest tombolo in England. As well as connecting Portland to the mainland the rocks and pebbles of the beach protect the softer rocks behind from erosion. One estimate states that without Chesil Beach coastal erosion would have reached Dorchester by now. The stretch of water behind the beach is known as the Fleet and provides a valuable habitat for seabirds. During World War II the Fleet was used for the testing of Barnes-Wallace's bouncing bomb.

WORBARROW TOUT *(right)*

Worbarrow Tout is the name of the headland that protects Worbarrow Bay. The name "tout" means "a lookout". Erosion has exposed the Purbeck limestones and shales on the cliffs so that dinosaur footprints and many types of fossils including the remains of crocodile and shark have been found here. The beach at Worbarrow Bay is difficult to reach but is highly appreciated by local people for its sheltered location and steep shelf that gives quick access to deep water. The same features make the beach popular with small boats which can anchor close to the shore.

LYME REGIS

Set in the heart of the Jurassic Coast where the cliffs of Dorset meet the valleys or "coombes" of Devon, Lyme Regis has a location which many describe as the most beautiful bay in Britain. The quaint town nestles under the steep slopes of Timber Hill and along the seafront eye-catching views of the Heritage Coast and beyond are usually visible including Golden Cap, Portland Bill and Chesil Beach. Visitors usually make a beeline to Lyme's quaint old harbour with its throng of boats and the famous harbour wall or "Cobb" immortalised both in Jane Austen's *Persuasion* and John Fowles' *The French Lieutenant's Woman*. Beatrix Potter stayed in the town and loved it so much that many of the town's whitewashed cottages appear as backdrops to her famous children's book illustrations.